145 Wonderful
Writing Prompts
from Favorite Literature

by
Susan Ohanian

S C H O L A S T I C
PROFESSIONAL **B**OOKS

New York • Toronto • London • Auckland • Sydney
Mexico City • New Delhi • Hong Kong

Cover design by Drew Hires
Interior design by Carmen R. Sorvillo

ISBN 0-590-01973-2

Printed in the U.S.A.

Table of Contents

Introduction

Writing cannot be divorced from reading. Children learn to read by reading; it is also the way they learn to write. In order to convince children to spend time with books, we need to convince them that reading is worth their while, to show them they will find insight and pleasure in books. The 145 prompts in these pages, chosen from books children love, are a good way to get started.

Start the day with a provocative prompt, inviting class discussion for, say, ten minutes. That will get the ideas percolating and later in the day students can continue the discussion in small groups or write a reflection on the prompt and ensuing discussion.

Since prior knowledge is crucial in both reading comprehension and the ability to find pleasure in books, these prompts are organized around themes that children care a lot about, such as Family Matters; Fitting In; Friendship; and Parents, Teachers, and Other Adults. These are small pieces from great literature that *speak* to children in a language they know, about ideas that are important to them.

These prompts are offered as a stimulus for
- provoking thinking
- inspiring group discussion
- focusing student writing
- leading to further reading

Experience in my own classrooms has shown me that offering prompts like this influences childrens' reading and writing in ways that are at once powerful and mysterious. Children have a way of returning again and again to important things. They will raid libraries for miles around to find all the books by an author whose snippet astounds them. And literary echoes will pop up in their writing months after the initial exposure. Experienced teachers know that good things have staying power in our classrooms, and these literary gems are most definitely something good.

Selection Sources

* indicates a book is out of print

Adventure and Survival

He was sitting in a bushplane roaring seven thousand feet above the northern wilderness with a pilot who had suffered a massive heart attack and who was either dead or in something close to a coma. He was alone.
In the roaring plane with no pilot he was alone.
Alone.

—from *Hatchet*, a Newbery Honor Book, by Gary Paulsen

- What would you do if you were the only passenger in a plane and the pilot fell into a coma?
- If you survived a plane crash in the mountain wilderness, what five things would you want to have with you?
- What five things would you want to have if you were left stranded on an island off the coast of Florida?

I built the fence first because it was too cold to sleep on the rock and I did not like to sleep in the shelter I had made until I was safe from the wild dogs. . . . I used the rock for the back of the house and the front I left open since the wind did not blow from this direction. The poles I made of equal length, using fire to cut them as well as a stone knife which caused me much difficulty because I had never made such a tool before. . . .
The winter was half over before I finished the house, but I slept there and felt secure because of the strong fence. The foxes came when I was cooking my food and stood outside gazing through the cracks, and the wild dogs also came, gnawing at the whale ribs, growling because they could not get in.

—from *Island of the Blue Dolphins*, a Newbery Medal Book, by Scott O'Dell

- Karana was left behind on the island as a young girl. If you were in her position, what would be harder for you—trying to build shelter and find food or facing your own fear? Explain how the strengths and weaknesses that you possess would help and hurt you.
- What else would you advise Karana to do to survive on the island?

. . . she decided that her leaving home would not just be running from something but would be running to something. To a large place, a comfortable place, an indoor place, and preferably a beautiful place. And that's why she decided upon the Metropolitan Museum of Art in New York City.

She planned very carefully; she saved her allowance and she chose her companion. She chose Jamie, the second youngest of her three younger brothers. He could be counted on to be quiet, and now and then he was good for a laugh. Besides, he was rich. . . . He saved almost every penny he got.

—from *From the Mixed-Up Files of Mrs. Basil E. Frankweiler,* a Newbery Medal Book, by E. L. Konigsburg

- What do you think of the girl's plan to run away? Will she be successful? Has she forgotten anything?
- Write a letter of advice to a friend planning to run away from home.

By the next morning the tight place in his stomach was gone. By the morning after that Matt decided that it was mighty pleasant living alone.

He enjoyed waking to a day stretched before him to fill as he pleased. He could set himself the necessary chores without having to listen to any advice about how they should be done. . . . To cook a meal for himself once or twice a day, he had to keep a fire going. Twice in the first few days he had waked and found the ashes cold. . . . Back home in Quincy, if his mother's fire burned out she had sent him or Sarah with her shovel to borrow a live coal from a neighbor. There was no neighbor here. He had to gather twigs and make a wad of shredded cedar bark, then strike his flint and blow on the tiny spark until it burst into flame. A man could get mighty hungry before he coaxed that spark into a cooking fire.

—from *The Sign of the Beaver,* a Newbery Honor Book, by Elizabeth George Speare

- What special dangers do you think ten-year-olds faced on their own one hundred or more years ago?
- The hero of *The Sign of the Beaver* thinks that it is "mighty pleasant living alone." What would you like about being on your own?
- Which would be harder, being home alone one hundred years ago or today?

The first blast of wind struck him as he made for the top of the cleft. It battered against his body and ripped at his clothing, and he had to cling to a projecting crag to keep from being flung from the mountainside.

—from *Banner in the Sky*, a Newbery Honor Book, by James Ramsey Ullman

- This is the story of a sixteen-year-old boy who is determined to climb a dangerous mountain. Why do you think people risk their lives climbing mountains?
- Would you describe yourself as someone who likes to take risks such as climbing a dangerous mountain? Use examples to show whether or not you're a risk taker.

Not every thirteen-year-old girl is accused of murder, brought to trial, and found guilty. But I was just such a girl, and my story is worth relating even if it did happen years ago. Be warned, however, this is no Story of a Bad Boy, *no* What Katy Did. *If strong ideas and action offend you, read no more. Find another companion to share your idle hours. For my part I intend to tell the truth as I lived it.*

—from *The True Confessions of Charlotte Doyle*, a Newbery Honor Book, by Avi

- The books Charlotte Doyle mentions are about "bad kids." She seems to suggest that these books aren't true, that the kids in them aren't really bad. Do you believe that there are "bad kids"?
- What bad kids have you read about? What good kids have you read about?

Three days later, when I had convinced myself that my parents had forgotten all about my plan and that I'd have to make another plea, they surprised me by telling me that I could go. . . .There were, however, conditions.

—from *Chasing Redbird* by Sharon Creech

- Zinnia, a 13-year-old girl, feels there are too many kids in her Kentucky farmhouse. She wants a place of her own and proposes spending the summer clearing a trail in the wilds, camping along the trail at night. One of her parents' conditions is that she has to come home every ten days so they know she is all right. What other conditions do you think Zinnia's parents have?
- List the things you'd carry on a ten-day stay in the woods.

If I went back now, or tried to, I would always be Moss, the boy who stayed a boy, to myself as well as to everyone else. . . .

Since I couldn't go back, since I couldn't stay where I was, I had to go forward. The way home, if there was one, was to walk ahead, to discover a new road that would belong to no one but me, to find my way out through a different door than the one I had entered.

—from *Guests* by Michael Dorris

- Describe a "new road" that you've taken in your own life.
- Moss has three choices—he can go back, stay where he is, or go forward. Discuss his choices in terms of past, present, and future. Share a situation when you were at a crossroads in your own life.

Lucy felt a little frightened, but she felt very inquisitive and excited as well. She looked back over her shoulder and there, between the dark tree-trunks, she could still see the open doorway of the wardrobe and even catch a glimpse of the empty room from which she had set out. . . . "I can always get back if anything goes wrong," thought Lucy.

—from *The Lion, the Witch and the Wardrobe* by C. S. Lewis

- When exploring a big, old house, Lucy walks into a wardrobe and discovers Narnia, a strange new country. Put yourself in Lucy's position. How would you have felt about the discovery? Tell what you would have done. For instance, would you have gone into Narnia or would you have shut the wardrobe door?
- Lucy believes that she'll be able to "get back if anything goes wrong." What do you think?
- Begin your own adventure story. Have someone go through some kind of opening—a door, a window, a hole in the ground—and fall into some kind of adventure.

Being with Older People

 *"She dribbles cranberry sauce on her dress, and she talks with her mouth full. I hate that."*

Her mother didn't say anything.

"And she forgets my name. I hate that, too."

Her mother didn't say anything. She put mashed potatoes into a yellow bowl. Anastasia started to cry. A salt-flavored tear came down the side of her face and into the corner of her mouth; she tasted it with the tip of her tongue, and waited for the next one.

"I don't hate grandmother," she said in a voice that had to find its way out lopsided around the tears. "But I hate it that she's so old."

"It makes my heart hurt."

—from *Anastasia Krupnik* by Lois Lowry

- Think about the older people you know. What do they do well, and what do they have trouble doing?
- How do you think Anastasia's grandmother feels about getting old?

That first night . . . with OB and May was as close to paradise as I may ever come in my life. Paradise because these two old people—who never dreamed they'd be bringing a little girl back from their visit with the relatives in Ohio—started . . . to turn their rusty, falling-down place into a house just meant for a kid. . . . I saw Oreos and Ruffles and big bags of Snickers. Those little cardboard boxes of juice that I had always, just once, wanted to try. I saw fat bags of marshmallows and cans of SpaghettiOs and a little plastic bear full of honey.

—from *Missing May*, a Newbery Medal Book, by Cynthia Rylant

- Do you think older people are more likely to give kids food they like rather than food that's "good for them"? Present your reasoning, and give an example to back it up.
- What foods would you like to see when you opened your kitchen cabinets and the refrigerator?

> *Uncle David is old. So old we don't even know for sure how old he is. He says when he dies he wants to be thrown on the manure pile just like the dead animals, but he might be kidding.*

—from *The Winter Room*, a Newbery Honor Book, by Gary Paulsen

- Describe a time when it was hard for you to tell if an older person was kidding or not.
- What's your definition of "old" when you talk about someone like Uncle David? For instance, at what age does someone become "old"? Can someone who is young in years be considered "old"?

> *"Come, come," yelled Uncle Wrisby. "We'll have something to eat. Then we'll talk about the world and its workings." He took hold of Arthur's hand. "What would you like to talk about?"*
> *Arthur stared at Uncle Wrisby. Here was someone who wanted to talk about things! With him!*

—from *Arthur, For the Very First Time*, an ALA Notable Children's Book, by Patricia MacLachlan

- Do you enjoy talking with older people and other adults? Tell why or why not.
- What are some of your favorite things to talk about? Express whether or not you feel that an older person would be interested in the same things.

> *Amitabha! Bandit was in trouble, deep trouble. Grandmother was the Matriarch of the House of Wong. What she ordered was always done. What she said was always so. . . . No one ever disobeyed the Matriarch.*

—from *In the Year of the Boar and Jackie Robinson*, by Bette Bao Lord

- What do you think of everyone in a family obeying an elderly grandmother?
- How do American families regard the opinions of their grandmothers?
- Do you think an elderly grandmother should be obeyed, no matter what? Give at least two examples to defend your view.

By now I figured that Grandpa's dirty tricks weren't over yet. I was right. All of my flannel shirts hanging on hangers in my closet were still hanging there, but they had been turned inside out. I grabbed one and fixed it and put it on. . . . My jeans hanging on a hook by a belt loop were inside out too. I fixed them and put them on, then saw that my belt was missing. The heck with it, I thought. I was too late to worry about a little thing like a belt.

That's when I discovered that there were no laces in my sneakers.

—from *The War with Grandpa* by Robert Kimmel Smith

- When a grandson declares war on his grandfather (over a bedroom in the house), who do you think will win? Tell why.
- If you were the grandson in the story, tell how you would respond to your grandfather's actions.

"I thought what you did was wonderful, Andy. I'm proud of you."

"What he did, coach, was garbage," Grampa snapped. "You play the game to win. There's no other reason to play."

"I don't agree, Mr. Harris," Mr. Cartwright said quietly. "There are things as important as winning, and good sportsmanship is among them. I think Andy showed that."

"He showed crap," Grampa said, and spat. . . . "There was no way that kid could have tagged you out, Andy. He didn't even know he had the ball. All you had to do was bang into him."

"I could've hurt him, Grampa. . . . Tubby's my friend. . . ."

"You don't have friends on the other team when you're in a ball game. . . . A game's something you play to win. There's no other point in playin'."

—from *The Trading Game* by Alfred Slote

- Who do you agree with, Grampa or the coach? Explain why you do or do not believe that winning is everything.
- Tell which is harder to do, and why: argue with a parent or a grandparent.

Maxine had put on a purple fake-fur coat with a red-striped belt around the waist. Her hat was black velvet, the kind old ladies wear to church, with a big gold pin on the front. Her gloves were yellow and pink, and she had a red plastic pocketbook over her arm.

—from *Crazy Lady,* a Newbery Honor Book, by Jane Leslie Conly

- Neighborhood kids make fun of Maxine. Vernon, a seventh grader in danger of failing, has agreed to help Maxine clean her yard in exchange for tutoring from a former teacher he likes. Why would it be so hard for a seventh grade boy to be seen with an eccentric woman like Maxine? Do you think it would it be easier for a girl? Would it be easier for a younger child? Explain your thinking.
- Write a description of what you might look like when you're 70 years old.

Grandfather sighed. "I don't know. Everything's changing, and I don't like it."
"Me, either. I don't like it at all."
Suddenly Grandfather laughed. "Come now, Thomas. It's all right for a grandparent to grumble about change, but not someone your age. Do you want to be a ten-year-old fogey?"
"I want things to be the way they were before—I mean, the way they once were."

—from *Stealing Home* by Mary Stolz

- Who do you think handles change better, an older person or a younger person? Explain your answer.
- How do you feel about change? Give an example to make your point.

Family Matters

> *I asked my mom if I was adopted and she about died laughing. "Whatever made you ask that?" she said (when she finally stopped laughing about ten hours later). "No, you're not adopted." I was a little disappointed when she said that, and then I got to thinking that maybe she wouldn't want to tell me the truth, so maybe I am adopted, but I'll never really know unless she plans to tell me the truth when I'm sixteen. Actually, I've often suspected that I am adopted.*
>
> —from *Absolutely Normal Chaos* by Sharon Creech

- Why do many kids suspect that they're adopted? Tell whether or not you've ever felt that way.
- Why do you think the mom in the passage above had such a good laugh?
- Describe a situation from your own life when you were being serious and your parents thought you were being funny.

> *"Hey, listen, let me explain the unwritten parental rule." Russell leaned forward.... "This is what they say, what all parents tell themselves before they go to bed at night." He raised his eyebrows. "Here it is: "What I don't know won't hurt me."*
> *"They don't say that."*
> *"Sure they do. See, Mom and Dad don't care if we pull a joke as long as they don't have to hear about it. And the one I have in mind that's a guaranteed simple-to-fix-before-they-get-home practical joke. They'll never, ever know.*
>
> —from *The Practical Joke War* by Alane Ferguson

- Challenge or defend Russell's belief that parents don't want to know certain things that their kids may be doing.
- How do you feel about practical jokes? Give a real-life example that illustrates your feeling about practical jokes.

When something bad happens, people don't all act the same way. Some people go nuts and others just act like nothing has happened at all.

I always used to wonder which kind of person I was. Now I know.

I'm the kind who goes nuts.

I started going nuts that day after my father told me about the divorce. My mother knocked on my door at the regular time to get me up for school.

"Are you awake, Charles?" she yelled. I didn't answer. I must admit, I was getting pretty good at not answering. It's really very easy. All you have to do is not open your mouth.

To me, the greatest thing about not answering is that no one can make you do it if you don't want to. That makes it very special. Because when you think about it, there're not too many things your parents can't make you do it if they really try hard enough.

—from *Don't Make Me Smile* by Barbara Park

- Charles gets revenge against his parents by not talking. What other things do kids do to get revenge against adults?
- What kind of person are you—do you go nuts or do you act like nothing has happened at all? List two things that are positive and two things that are negative about your behavior when something bad happens.

Dear Denise,

My problem is my family. I am thirteen. I have an older sister, who is eighteen; a brother, seventeen; a little brother, eight years old, and a little sister, six. We fight all the time, especially at the dinner table.

And then our parents get mad and start fighting, too. I'd really like to change this. What can I do?

Signed: Tired of Family Karate

—from *Family Karate* by Kathryn Ewing

- If you were Denise the advice columnist, what advice would you give to "Tired of Family Karate"?
- Which child are you—oldest, middle, youngest, or an only child? How do you think your position in the family affects your life?

Like most grown-ups, Sam Kellow's parents never guessed that their son ever thought about money. Like most grown-ups, they thought he did not appreciate its value, and they both liked to say things to him like "Money doesn't grow on trees" and "If you knew how much that cost, you wouldn't do that."

—from *The Big Bazoohley* by Peter Carey

- What are some of the things that you've heard adults say about money?
- For one day, keep a record of when you think about money, and what your thoughts about it are.

Birch sighed, "Pop, I'm not a child. I'm thirteen. You're just like Mom. If Mom wants me to make a salad, she goes, 'Walk to the refrigerator. Open the door. Reach down. Open the crisper. Take out the lettuce. . . .' But she doesn't always tell me important things."

—from *Coast to Coast*, an American Bookseller Pick of the List and IRA Children's Choice Book, by Betsy Byars

- What things are important for a parent to tell a child? How old should a child be when a parent explains each thing?
- What are some things that your parents tell you, step-by-step, to do? Explain whether or not you feel that they need to explain every step.

The Quimby women, as Mr. Quimby referred to his wife and daughters, were enthusiastic about Mr. Quimby's decision to give up smoking. He was less enthusiastic because, after all, he was the one who had to break the habit.

Ramona took charge. She collected all her father's cigarettes and threw them in the garbage. . . .

—from *Ramona and Her Father*, a Newbery Honor Book, by Beverly Cleary

- Discuss a bad habit that you broke, or tried to break.
- Do you agree with Ramona's anti-smoking method? Can you think of other ways to help an adult quit smoking? Create your own anti-smoking plan.

> ***Mr. Martin shakes his head, "You two are impossible. You should be happy to help out, to be part of the family. The only reason for a baby-sitter is that your mother and I won't be home until very late and we don't think it's safe to leave the two of you home alone, without a referee.***

—from *Everyone Else's Parents Said Yes* by Paula Danziger

- Why do you think Mr. and Mrs. Martin felt their kids needed a referee?
- At what age do you think kids can be left home alone? Give your reasons for choosing this age.
- At what age do you think someone can start babysitting? Tell why you picked this age.

> ***I have three brothers—born bad—who can get away with average report cards with D's in math. Who have tried cigarettes. . . .Who lie to my parents straight-faced. Every Saturday, Sammy packs his book bag and says he's off to the library (which is located in Cassie Starr's basement) to study math, which, according to Nicho, he does between kiss-es. And my parents never think to ask why he gets D's in trigonometry if he studies in the library every Saturday. . . .***
> ***I have had no choice. I am the fourth child, and a girl to boot. I have had to take what was left and say thank you. I promise you, given half a chance, I would not have chosen to be good.***

—from *The Bad Dreams of a Good Girl* by Susan Shreve

- Tell whether or not you agree with this statement: Third- or fourth-born children usually have to take what is left.
- Make a list of things you think girls get away with. Then list the things boys get away with. Compare your two lists. Who gets away with more?
- Write a paragraph to answer the following question: Can a person choose whether or not to be good or bad?

Al suffers a lot from role reversal. I think having no father around or any kind of sibling, she sometimes feels as if she's her mother's mother and has to take care of her. I guess a lot of kids who live with just their mothers get into that habit.

—from *Al(exandra) the Great* by Constance C. Greene

- Do you agree with the above narrator? Make an argument about whether or not most kids worry a lot about their parents.
- How do you feel about the following statement: Kids worry as much about their parents as parents worry about their kids.

Funny thing was, I used to like Porter Dotson fine when he was just the feller down the street who ran the newspaper. He was funny and friendly. Then he married my mama two years ago, and I stopped liking him. Every time I saw him sitting there where my daddy used to sit reading the paper by the picture window, I wanted to shout at him, "Move your carcass outa my daddy's place!"

But instead, I didn't say anything at all, sometimes for days on end. Even if he asked me a point-blank question, I wouldn't answer him. Yeah, it was wicked of me. I enjoyed seeing that bewildered look come over his face.

—from *Belle Prater's Boy*, a Newbery Honor Book, by Ruth White

- Explain why kids may sometimes treat their stepparents so unfairly.
- If you were Porter Dotson, what would you do? Write a dialogue between Porter and his stepson.

Without another word I walked away and went into my own room. It's so small you can hardly turn around in it. But one nice thing is that out of my window I can see part of the park and a nice chunk of sky.

—from *Going Home* by Nicholasa Mohr

- What are the best and worst things about your bedroom?
- Describe in words and drawings what your ideal bedroom would look like.

> *"Perhaps he thought he was the only one."*
> *Ralph's voice was thick with scorn. "How could he think he was the only one? Stories from the old days are knee-deep in stepmothers and stepfathers!"*
> *Claudia picked up the little wooden cow and stroked its nose. "Everyone thinks that they're the only one. You ought to know that."*
>
> —from *Step by Wicked Step* by Anne Fine

- What does Ralph mean when he says, "Stories from the old days are knee-deep in stepmothers and stepfathers!"?
- Is Claudia right? Does every child whose parents get divorced, every child who doesn't like living with stepparents and stepbrothers and sisters, think he or she is the only one? Write a letter of advice to a stepchild.

> *In 1864 Caddie Woodlawn was eleven, and as wild a little tomboy as ever ran the woods of western Wisconsin. She was the despair of her mother and of her elder sister, Clara. But her father watched her with a little shine of pride in his eyes, and her brothers accepted her as one of themselves without a question. Indeed, Tom who was two years older, and Warren, who was two years younger than Caddie, needed Caddie to link them together into an inseparable trio.*
>
> —from *Caddie Woodlawn*, a Newbery Medal Book, by Carol Ryrie Brink

- Do you believe that brothers and sisters got along better in the past than they do today? Defend your answer.
- If you're a girl, do you identify with Caddie Woodlawn? If you're a boy, would you like to have Caddie as a friend? Tell why or why not.

Fitting In

I didn't know Maudie that well . . . I didn't have to know her to know I didn't want to get stuck doing anything with her. Maudie was sort of a dope—one of those kids that everybody wants to avoid. It's not that you get together and vote on that kind of thing, but you know. It's hard to explain. There's usually something different about the person, like wearing socks instead of tights or tights instead of socks—whichever's the opposite of what most kids do.

—from *Maudie and Me and the Dirty Book* by Betty Miles

- Are there certain clothing "rules" in your school about the kinds of clothes you need to wear to be accepted? Define the rules.
- What can an adult do to help a kid that other kids avoid—or do adults make things worse?
- Do you like to read books about kids who are misfits—or books about kids who are the most popular kids in their school? Explain your choice.

They say Maniac Magee was born in a dump. They say his stomach was a cereal box and his head a sofa spring.

They say he kept an eight-inch cockroach on a leash and that rats stood guard over him while he slept.

They say if you knew he was coming and you sprinkled salt on the ground and he ran over it, within two or three blocks he would be as slow as everybody else.

They say.

—from *Maniac Magee*, a Newbery Medal Book, by Jerry Spinelli

- Do you personally know anyone who seems to be "larger than life" like the legendary Maniac Magee?
- Invent a legend about yourself. Begin by making up three "They say" statements about yourself.

> *"I don't think people like people who are different."*
>
> —from *Do Bananas Chew Gum?*, a Carl Sandburg Award Book,
>   by Jamie Gilson

- Do you agree with the quote above? Do you believe that people really want everybody to be the same? Be sure to justify your response.
- Should kids who are different, or who feel as if they are different, try to change? Explain your views.

> *It had been an unhappy morning for [Louis]. He felt frightened at being different. He couldn't understand why he had come into the world without a voice. Everyone else seemed to have a voice. Why didn't he? "Fate is cruel," he thought. "Fate is cruel to me."*
>
> —from *Trumpet of the Swan* by E. B. White

- Team up with a buddy and make a list of all the ways you two are alike and all the ways you are different from each other. Which list is longer?
- Describe one thing that is unique about each person in the class.

> *Of course, he was far from perfect yet. At dinner his father told him not to slurp his soup. His mother told him to quit eating so fast. And his sister told him to put his feet on his own side of the table.*
> *Milo couldn't stand it. "I bet you'd love me if I turned perfect," he said.*
>
> —from *Be a Perfect Person in Just Three Days!* by Stephen Manes

- Make a list of what you feel you would need to do to get your family to think you were perfect.
- What's your idea of a perfect person? Draw a word web for the word perfect.
- Write down four suggestions that would make the world a better place. How does your personal list compare to this list?

Being the fattest kid in the fifth grade is not easy. And the nickname that Phil Steinkraus hung on me has stuck. Even Libby Klein, this very nice girl who lives around the corner and is in my class, even Libby calls me Jelly Belly once in a while. I guess she and the other kids figure that I don't mind that name too much. Or that I don't care.

I do care. It hurts me a lot.

—from *Jelly Belly* by Robert Kimmel Smith

- Imagine a conversation between Phil and Nathaniel, the narrator of the above passage.
- Why do you think kids like Phil make up hurtful nicknames for people?

In the back of the room she saw a chart that listed the name of every student in the class who has a row of gold stars. Next to 'Bradley Chalkers,' there were no gold stars.

—from *There's a Boy in the Girl's Bathroom,*
an IRA-CBA Children's Choice Book by Louis Sachar

- How do you think a kid who never gets a gold star feels?
- Evaluate the use of gold stars. Do gold stars and other rewards make kids work harder? Can such rewards have negative results?
- If someone like Bradley, who never received a gold star, were in your class, what would you do to make him feel better?

We were the leftovers. The scrubs. There were seven of us—four boys and three girls. The seven who nobody wanted.

That was fine with me!

So what if I wasn't very good? So what if the ball didn't always roll where I kicked it? So what if I tripped over my own big feet or forgot and used my hands sometimes? I didn't care!

Only, I really did.

—from *Never Say Quit* by Bill Wallace

- What's your advice for a sixth grader who is no good at sports—in a school where sports are very important?
- If you were the coach or teacher in *Never Say Quit,* how would you make sure the leftovers got placed on teams?

"I want you to be the best you can be. Just so you remember that God don't judge you by the number of stars you get. . . . I want something for you, Lena. For all my children. And I hope I'm not wrong, because it's going to cost you pain, but I want it for you just the same. I want you not to know your place. You have a right to an education and hope and the chance to use your gifts. I pray to God you won't ever have to live your life by somebody else's rules.

—from *Words By Heart,* an IRA Children's Book Award Book
by Ouida Sebestyen

- In the passage above, Lena's father is talking to her. What does her dad mean when he says that he doesn't want her to know her place or live by somebody else's rules?
- Which do you feel that schools should do: Teach kids to know their place or teach them how to make their own rules? Tell why.

There's nothing more embarrassing than shooting your hand in the air to vote for something and then finding out that it's up there waving all alone. Drew says it makes you look like an individual. But I think it just makes you look like you've got bad taste.

—from *Beanpole* by Barbara Park

- How does voting with the majority prove that somebody has "good" taste?
  What makes voting in the minority "bad" taste?
- Suppose you were the only one voting for something. How would you feel? Would you want to change your vote?

"So today's the first day of the fourth grade," he said, "the year they separate the sheep from the goats."

—from *Keep Ms. Sugarman in the Fourth Grade* by Elizabeth Levy

- What does the narrator mean?
- Explain how schools separate people.

Last year, in seventh grade, the last thing I wanted to be was weird. Being ordinary, normal, that was my plan. Which I knew was gonna be hard, because I have the weirdest family in the world, and that kind of stuff is bound to rub off.

But I was determined to be normal like other kids. Normal enough so that I'd blend into the blah-brown walls of the junior high. Normal enough so I'd never get laughed at or picked on. . . .

—from *Seventh-Grade Weirdo* by Lee Wardlaw

- Why do you think the narrator feels it's so important to blend in?
- Do you prefer to blend in or to stand out? Illustrate your response with a real situation from your life.

All my life I thought I had lived in a safe, warm, secure world where I was just like everyone else, but it had only been my little fantasy. I looked too Chinese. And yet, even if I learned Chinese and the culture, I looked too American. There would always be someone like Dwight to call me a half-breed.

I felt . . . lost.

—from *Thief of Hearts* by Laurence Yep

- What are the advantages and disadvantages of having parents of different races?
- Share your idea of what a "safe, warm, secure world" would be like.

"Wanda," she'd say, giving one of her friends a nudge, "tell us. How many dresses did you say you had hanging up in your closet?

"A hundred," said Wanda.

"A hundred!" exclaimed all the girls incredulously, and the little girls would stop playing hopscotch and listen.

"Yeah, a hundred, all lined up," said Wanda. Then her thin lips drew together in silence.

"Yeah, velvet too. A hundred dresses," repeated Wanda stolidly. "All lined up in my closet."

Then they'd let her go. And then before she'd gone very far, they couldn't help bursting into shrieks and peals of laughter.

A hundred dresses! Obviously the only dress Wanda had was the blue one she wore every day. So what did she say she had a hundred for?

—from *The Hundred Dresses*, a Newbery Honor Book, by Eleanor Estes

- Evaluate which you think is worse, Wanda's lies or the behavior of her classmates.
- Why do you think Wanda tells the story of the hundred dresses?

Juliet knew the things people said about her. Some kids called her bossy, just because she pointed out the right way to do things. Some kids called her nosy, just because she helped Mrs. Lacey see when someone wasn't working. Some people called her "The Announcer," just because she mentioned other people's mistakes.

But Juliet knew the truth. She knew she was motivated. That's what her mother said she was—motivated. And that was what Juliet needed to be if she was going to grow up to be a doctor. To be a doctor you had to do things right. And you had to start early.

—from *Juliet Fisher and the Foolproof Plan* by Natalie Honeycutt

- Explain whether or not you think that Juliet will be a good doctor when she grows up.
- Write a letter of advice to Juliet about her behavior.

 *Another thing about Admiral Peary—he'd been a boy kind of like Martin. Misbehaving all over the place. In fights with his peers, in dutch with his teachers, in trouble with the neighbors.*

—from *The Explorer of Barkham Street* by Mary Stolz

- Martin is a lonely boy. Why do you think he likes to read about Arctic explorers such as Admiral Peary?
- Imagine what Martin will be like as a man. Write a paragraph describing his accomplishments— or lack of them.

The world revolves around my sister, Allie.
Okay, maybe not the whole world. But our corner of it does.
You see, Allie is the Allison Burrows, the best softball pitcher in the state of California. Anyone who knows anything about fast-pitch softball knows Allie.
Nobody knows me. I'm Molly Burrows, the ten-year-old shadow of the great Allie.

—from *A Season of Comebacks* by Kathy Mackel

- In your opinion, who does the world revolve around in your corner? Explain why this person is the center of attention.
- What would you advise Molly to do to stop being "the ten-year-old shadow of the great Allie"?

I think how you look is the most important thing in the world. If you look cute, you are cute; if you look smart, you are smart, and if you don't look like anything, then you aren't anything.

—from *The Summer of the Swans*, a Newbery Award Book, by Betsy Byars

- Sara, a fourteen year old girl, believes that the way you look is who you are. Based on what she says, do you think Sara believes that people can change the way they look? Use an example to state your case.
- How do you think you look today?

Flights of Fantasy

"Ya wanna fight?" he demanded.

"Why?" The kitten put down his crust, and simply asked, "Why?"

"Well—well—" Tucker Mouse was flustered. "It's just that—well—cats and mice fight. That's all."

"But why?" the kitten continued to question. "I was starving to death before I found this pitiful piece of sandwich. Some overfed human being missed that garbage can, so I got to eat. And you don't look too beefy yourself. So why make life worse for each other by fighting?"

Tucker Mouse was somewhat taken aback. He hadn't expected such reasonable talk from a skinny kitten sitting next to a trash can and a decaying pumpkin.

"But—what do we do if we don't fight?" asked Tucker.

"Mmm—" The kitten purred softly, like a philosopher. "We could just be friends. . . . I know that it's unusual," said the kitten. "At least, I know it's supposed to be. But this is New York! And all the rules are broken here. For the best, I hope. We might even set a precedent.

—from *Harry Kitten and Tucker Mouse* by George Selden

- What rules do you think need to be broken? What new ways of thinking need to be encouraged?
- What other animals aren't supposed to get along with each other? Write a story about the friendship between two animals who are supposed to be enemies.

Ralph was an unusual mouse. He had listened to so many children and watched so much television that he had learned to talk. Not everyone could understand him. Those who could were lonely children who shared Ralph's interest in fast cars and motorcycles and who took the trouble to listen.

—from *Ralph S. Mouse* by Beverly Cleary

- What would you say to a mouse who could talk?
- In this story, Ralph enjoys staying at a boy's school. What could he do for fun at your school?

"The real point is this: We don't know where to go because we don't know what we are. Do you want to go back to living in a sewer-pipe? And eating other people's garbage? Because that's what rats do. But the fact is, we aren't rats any more. We're something Dr. Schultz has made. Something new. Dr. Schultz says our intelligence has increased more than one thousand per cent. I suspect he's underestimated; I think we're probably as intelligent as he is—maybe more. We can read, and with a little practice, we'll be able to write, too. I mean to do both. I think we can learn to do anything we want. But where do we do it? Where does a group of civilized rats fit in?"

—from *Mrs. Frisby and the Rats of NIMH*, a Newbery Medal Book, by Robert C. O'Brien

- In the above passage, Nicodemus, the intelligent rat leader is speaking. How would you answer Nicodemus's last two questions?
- What would you do if you discovered Nicodemus and the other rats in your home?

"Not many creatures can spin webs. Even men aren't as good at it as spiders, although they think they're pretty good, and they'll try anything. Did you ever hear of the Queensborough Bridge?"

Wilbur shook his head. "Is it a web?"

"Sort of," replied Charlotte. "But do you know how long it took men to build it? Eight whole years. My goodness, I would have starved to death waiting that long. I can make a web in a single evening."

"What do people catch in the Queensborough Bridge—bugs?" asked Wilbur.

"No," said Charlotte. "They don't catch anything. They just keep trotting back and forth across the bridge thinking there is something better on the other side."

—from *Charlotte's Web* by E. B. White

- Study some pictures of bridges. Charlotte says bridges are sort of like webs. Use your own flight of fantasy to describe a particular bridge.
- Think about the different reasons that people cross bridges. For each reason, give an example of something that would be better on the other side.

"Do not let an unnatural sadness settle over you, Louis," said the cob. "Swans must be cheerful, not sad; graceful, not awkward; brave, not cowardly. Remember that the world is full of youngsters who have some sort of handicap that they must overcome. You apparently have a speech defect. I am sure you will overcome it, in time. There may even be some slight advantage, at your age, in not being able to say anything. It compels you to be a good listener. The world is full of talkers, but it is rare to find anyone who listens. And I assure you that you can pick up more information when you are listening than when you are talking."

"My father does quite a lot of talking himself," thought Louis.

—from *The Trumpet of the Swan* by E. B. White

- Who is the best listener that you know? What makes him or her such a good listener?
- Describe yourself in terms of being a listener or a talker.

"I don't know how you learned reading," Polo would say with envy, when Marco jumped up on the counter to see if Mrs. Neal had added cat food to her shopping list.

"I simply paid attention," said Marco, meaning that all the time he was using the litter box with newspaper there at the bottom, he was studying the letters and words. He was bound to learn a little something. Polo simply did his business and climbed out.

The reason Mr. and Mrs. Neal did not know their pets could talk was that, when Marco and Polo conversed, it sounded like meowing. They could meow in hundreds of different ways that the Neals could not distinguish at all: soft and loud; short and long; wavy meows; sharp meows; meows that started out high and got low; meows that started out low and got high. Plus seventy-six different kinds of purrs.

—from *The Grand Escape* by Phyllis Reynolds Naylor

- Phyllis Reynolds Naylor describes all sorts of meows—wavy, sharp, soft and loud. Write down as many descriptions of a cat's purr as you can. (You can substitute the sound another animal makes such as a dog's growl or parakeet's cheep.)
- How do people communicate with each other without talking?

"I've been doing a little research, reading time-travel books—Half Magic, Narnia stuff, A Wrinkle in Time, and The Time Machine. . . . And do you know what people in those books always forget?"

"Food," said Fred. "They never eat in those books."

"No, you Neanderthal," said Sam. "They never pack anything useful to take with them. Like King Arthur would have been amazed by this calculator. The Cheyenne would have been wowed by a walkman. . . . If we just take the right ordinary stuff, people will be convinced we're magic."

—from *Your Mother Was a Neanderthal* by Jon Scieszka

- If you could travel back in time, to what year and location would you travel? Share the reasons for your choice.
- For their journey back in time, Fred took a Swiss army knife, a water pistol, and a Walkman. Sam took pens, can openers, potato peelers, and lots of other gadgets. What would you take on a similar journey?

As a child I was teased by the other children and pestered by the grownups for never bringing a lunch of my own to school or eating the hot lunch provided. . . . My diet is largely composed of small rodents and insects. I can hardly lunch on grasshoppers before the eyes of several hundred ninth graders, so I prefer not to eat lunch at all. . . . If I were to eat human food I would lose the ability to fly, even the ability to transform to owl shape.

—from *Owl in Love* by Patrice Kindl

- The narrator is a girl who is really an owl. Imagine you were a boy or a girl who was an animal. What kind of animal lunch would you have? What would happen to you if you were to eat human food?
- What would be your response if one of your classmates started to eat a lunch of grasshoppers?

"Boofy and Beau were Beauty and Beast, you know—" She dropped her voice to an excited whisper. "The lady called Pumpkin was Cinderella. And Belle, of course—the lady playing cards—was the Sleeping Beauty."

"Oh," said James.

"And now you have seen them," Mildred went on in the same excited whisper, "you have actually seen them with your own eyes!" She paused. "Now very few people could say that, could they? . . .

"Where are we exactly?" said James.

Mildred frowned slightly and followed the direction of his eyes. "It's hard to explain. I mean"—she hesitated—"you remember it said that they all 'lived happily ever after'?"

—from *Are All the Giants Dead?* by Mary Norton

- If all the fairy tale characters lived happily ever after, imagine what your favorite character might be doing today. For instance, when James sees Cinderella, she's reading a gossip magazine.
- What does the phrase "lived happily ever after" mean to you?

Not long from now, in the Atomic Age, it is easy to imagine that travel will be tremendously fast. In order to travel, for example, from New York to Calcutta, you will simply have to walk into a station in New York, through one door into a room beamed on Calcutta, out another door into the station in Calcutta, then on out into Calcutta's streets. It will take you no longer than it takes you to walk through any ordinary room and you won't feel a thing.

—from *The 21 Balloons*, a Newbery Award Book, by William Pène du Bois

- What would be the advantages and disadvantages of such speedy travel?
- Take your own flight of fantasy. Devise a method of transportation for travel in the future. Choose two locations that are thousands of miles apart, and explain in detail how future travelers would get from one place to another quickly.

When you are young so many things are difficult to believe, and yet the dullest people will tell you that they are true—such things, for instance, as that the earth goes round the sun, and that it is not flat but round. The things that seem really likely, like fairy-tales and magic, are, so say the grown-ups, not true at all. Yet they are so easy to believe, especially when you see them happening.

—from *The Enchanted Castle* by E. Nesbit

• What fact that you know is harder to believe than any fairy tale you've read?
• Make up your own fairy tale or magical event.

Friendship

Ellie and Carolyn Oaks at school decided to be best friends. Ellie admired Carolyn because she had long red hair. Carolyn admired Ellie because she was thin. Neither of them wanted to be a sixth-grade cheerleader and neither of them had a boyfriend. And they both like dogs.

—from *A Blue-Eyed Daisy* by Cynthia Rylant

- Think about one of your friends. What do you admire about him or her?
- How important do you think it is that two friends like the same things? Do you believe that it's possible for two people with very different opinions to be good friends?

"I miss my brother William," said Sarah. . . . There are three old aunts who all squawk together like crows at dawn. I miss them, too."
"There are always things to miss," said Maggie. "No matter where you are."

—from *Sarah, Plain and Tall*, a Newbery Medal Book, by Patricia MacLachlan

- Explain what Maggie means when she says, "There are always things to miss."
- How would you help a friend who is missing another place and other people?

The summer started out as pure glory. My best friend Staci Hopper and I did all our favorite eleven-year-old girl things: biking, afternoon movies, and wandering through the mall looking at clothes too old for us.

—from *Polly Panic* by Mary Francis Shura

- What would be on your list of favorite things to do with your best friend?
- Name some things that are fun to do with a friend but that aren't as fun to do alone.

"What's your name?" she asked when she had stopped the rain of shells.

"Oats," he answered. "Oats Tiger."

She was about to laugh when she thought better of it. After all, her name was pretty funny, too. . . . Billie Wind concentrated her thoughts on her new friend.

"Oats," she said. "Well, that's an easy name to remember."

—from *The Talking Earth* by Jean Craighead George

- If Billie Wind had laughed at Oats Tiger's name, how do you suppose that might have affected their new friendship?
- Challenge or defend the following statement: You should always be completely honest with your friends and tell them exactly what you're thinking.

So now he had a buddy. They hung out in each other's carports, and lent each other gasoline for their lawn mowers when one of them ran out . . . . The one thing Jim wouldn't share were his afternoon visits to his alligator. For one thing, Buddy was a blabbermouth . . . .

—from *The Boy Who Loved Alligators* by Barbara Kennedy

- Do you have secrets from your best friend? Does your best friend keep secrets from you? What do you think would happen if you shared your secret?
- Jim says that Buddy is a blabbermouth. Challenge or defend the following statement: You can know someone's flaws and still be her or his friend. Give examples.

Wilbur never forgot Charlotte. Although he loved her children and her grandchildren dearly, none of the new spiders ever quite took her place in his heart. She was in a class by herself. It is not often that someone comes along who is a true friend and a good writer. Charlotte was both.

—from *Charlotte's Web*, a Newbery Honor Book, by E. B. White

- What does it take to be a true friend?
- Complete the sentence so it applies to a true friend of yours.

    _____ is a true friend and a good _____.

> *I don't have a whole lot of friends in my new school. Mom says maybe I'm a loner, but I don't know. A new boy in school has to be pretty cautious until he gets to know who's who. Maybe I'm just a boy nobody pays much attention to. . . .*
>
> *I wish somebody would ask me over some time. After school I stay around kicking a soccer ball with some of the other kids so they won't think I am stuck up or anything, but nobody asks me over.*
>
> —from *Dear Mr. Henshaw*, a Newbery Medal Book, by Beverly Cleary

- Offer fourth grader Leigh some advice on how to make friends in a new school. List three things a person might do to begin a friendship.
- List three things you could do to welcome a new student.
- What do you think Leigh means when he says, "A new boy in school has to be pretty cautious until he gets to know who's who."

> *"I don't think you or Onion John understands. . . . Please tell Onion John that the whole idea is to build him a regular, respectable house. There can't be any four bathtubs in the living room. Or five! Just one, tucked away in its own small room where maybe he'll enjoy using it more than once or twice a month." My father raised a finger. "Explain there's only going to be one bathtub in this house."*
>
> —from *Onion John*, a Newbery Medal Book, by Joseph Krumgold

- Onion John likes bathtubs. He uses one to store his beets and cabbages, another for onions and potatoes, another for dust, another for newspapers. When townspeople decide to build Onion John a house, it seems like a good, kind idea. But when you do something to help a person, who gets to decide just how things will go? For example, how many bathtubs should the new house have, and who should decide—the father or Onion John?

Jess roused himself and went to the front. As he passed Leslie's desk, she grinned and rippled her fingers low in a kind of wave. He jerked a nod. He couldn't help feeling sorry for her. It must be embarrassing to sit in front when you find yourself dressed funny on the first day of school. And you don't know anybody.

—from *Bridge to Terabithia*, a Newbery Medal Book, by Katherine Paterson

- Where do you and your friends like to sit in class—front or back? What are the advantages of your position?
- How important is it to you that you dress like everybody else? How important is it that your friends dress like everybody else?

Armand was angered . . . "You have taken my piece of the bridge."

"The bridges don't belong to anybody," said the woman. "They're the only free shelter in Paris."

Suzy tried to make peace. "He's a nice, friendly old tramp, mama," she explained, "and he's going to live with us."

"I'm not a friendly old tramp," said Armand indignantly. "I'm a mean, cranky old tramp, and I hate children and dogs and women."

"Then if you hate us," said Paul, "why did you give us some of your food?"

"Because I'm a stupid old tramp," replied Armand. "Because I'm a stupid, soft-hearted old tramp." Oh, la, la! There it was. He had let it slip that he really had a heart. Now this homeless family would surely be after that too.

—from *The Family Under the Bridge*, a Newbery Honor Book, by Natalie Savage Carlson

- What clues can you find that Armand has a softer heart than he wants to admit?
- Do you know anyone who has a "bark worse than his or her bite?" Use that person to illustrate what the phrase means.
- Why do some people resist making friends with someone who seems different?

Lots of Laughter

Pretty soon the food fight was in full swing. Everyone joined in. Ketchup and meatballs and mashed potatoes and French fries went flying. Cottage cheese and green Jell-O and applesauce sailed through the air and landed with lovely plops and splats.

—from *The Flying Substitute and Other Wacky School Stories* by Ellen Weiss & Mel Friedman

- What is funny about a food fight?
- Write a description of a food fight. Include the kinds of food you would use. Be sure to use language that tells how the food looks, tastes, sounds, feels, and smells.

When he opened the door, Arthur heard a clucking sound, but not like any clucking he had ever heard—it was deeper, louder. Arthur had a feeling that this wasn't going to work out.

He was right. Professor Mazzocchi came out of the apartment a few minutes later. He was leading a chicken that was taller than he was. "This is the best poultry bargain on earth," he said, "a medium sized superchicken—six cents a pound—here's your two hundred and sixty-six pound chicken, on the hoof. She'll be mighty good eating. Please don't forget to return the leash and collar," and Professor Mazzocchi closed the apartment door.

—from *The Hoboken Chicken Emergency* by Daniel Manus Pinkwater

- What would you do with a 266-pound chicken?
- Write a recipe for a dish made with a 266-pound chicken. Be sure to indicate how many pots and stoves you will need, how many people your recipe will serve, and what to do with the leftovers.

> *The Moron's Delight is one of Steve's specialties. It has six flavors of ice cream—two scoops of each—a banana, a carrot, three kinds of syrup, whole roasted peanuts, a slice of Swiss cheese, a radish, yogurt, wheat germ, and a kosher pickle. It is served in a shoebox lined with plastic wrap. Steve considers it a health-food dessert.*
>
> —from *The Magic Moscow* by Daniel Pinkwater

- Concoct your own "health-food dessert" that Steve might like. Be sure to give your dessert a name.
- Pretend that you write a column about food in the newspaper. Review the "Moron's Delight" in your column.

> *Class 6-A became a legend at My Dear Watson Elementary School. We were clever. We were sneaky. We were bad. We were very bad. We were a team. We had a plan. It was working.*
> *Five weeks passed. Seven substitute teachers had come, seen, and given up.*
>
> —from *Mister Fred* by Jill Pinkwater

- Why do students enjoy misbehaving when they have a substitute teacher?
- What kind of tricks have you played on a substitute teacher?

> *One time in science class, Goat got everybody to agree that when the teacher, Mr. Fellini, came back into the room, they would move their lips like they were answering his questions, only they wouldn't make any sound. That way, Goat said, Mr. Fellini would think he was going crazy and would go to the infirmary, leaving them free to have an extra recess.*
>
> —from *Cracker Jackson*, an ALA Notable Book, Parents' Choice Award Winner, and IRA-CBC Children's Choice Book by Betsy Byars

- What other things do kids do to try to trick their teachers?
- Why do you think students want to try to trick their teachers?

Then she saw it. Them. Two lumpy, repulsive, no-color things lying on the table side by side. Like something you would look away from if you saw it lying in a gutter. . . . "Nobody makes their kids eat parsnips! Listen, before you do another thing, Mom, call the Hot Line for Child Abuse. Confess to them that you were planning to feed parsnips to your children. They're there to help you, Mom."

—from *The One Hundredth Thing About Caroline* by Lois Lowry

- Write your own funny description of a food you hate.
- Tell about a time you would have called the Hot Line for Child Abuse after your mother or father wanted you to eat something you hated.

"My name's John Chapman, but folks call me Johnny Appleseed."

"Pleased to meet you," says Paul.

The little man points at his tree. "Mighty pretty sight, don't you think?"

"Sure is," says Paul, and with a quick-as-a-wink flick of his ax, he lays the tree out full length on the ground. "My name's Paul Bunyan."

The little man lifts his tin pot and wipes his bald head while he stares at the tree lying there in the dirt. Then he squints up at Paul and kneels down and puts another seed in the ground. Paul smiles down at him while the tree grows up, then he lays it out by the first. The little man pops three seeds into the ground fast as can be. Paul lets them come up, then he lops all three with one easy stroke, backhand.

"You sure make them come up fast," says Paul, admiring-like.

"It's a sort of a gift I was born with." says Johnny Appleseed. He looks at the five trees lying together. "You sure make them come down fast."

"It's a talent," says Paul, real humble. "I have to practice a lot."

—from *A Telling of the Tales: Five Stories* by William J. Brooke

- Team up with a partner and continue this tall tale conversation.
- What would happen if two other legends or characters crossed paths? Think of your favorite stories, or use some of the passages in this chapter.

I guess you've heard how amazing rich our farm is. Anything will grow in it—quick. Seeds burst in the ground, and crops shoot right up before your eyes. Why, just yesterday our oldest boy dropped a five-cent piece, and before he could find it, that nickel had grown to a quarter.

—from *McBroom's Wonderful One-Acre Farm* by Sid Fleischman

- Describe what would happen to at least two other things that you dropped in the soil at the McBroom's farm.
- Use your own yard or block as a location. Then relate an incredible event for that location—the more incredible, the better!

Parents, Teachers, and Other Adults

When Jerry's father saw Jerry's blue hair, his face turned beet red. "You have blue hair! How dare you have blue hair?"

"Hello, Father. Nice to see you, too," Jerry replied sarcastically.

"You have blue hair!"

"I know, Dad. I know."

Jerry's father started pacing back and forth. "No son of mine is going to be walking around town with blue hair. I have a reputation to think about. No one in my family has ever had blue hair."

"I didn't make my hair blue. . . . Ms. Merriweather did it, Dad."

"Who is she?"

"My new teacher," Jerry explained.

"Your teacher turned your hair blue?"

—from *They're Torturing Teachers in Room 104* by Jerry Piasecki

- What would you do if your teacher turned your hair blue? What would your parents do?
- With whom do you sympathize more, Jerry or his father? Explain why.
- What difference does it make what kind of hairstyle or haircolor a person has?

It had been clear to Minna at an early age—maybe seven—that her mother was different. She hated to cook, except for toast and hot oatmeal that she enjoyed stirring into a mass of beige lumps. She avoided cleaning. Minna's feet stuck to the kitchen floor sometimes, making sucking noises as she walked. You could eat off Emily Parmalee's mother's floor next door. Emily Parmalee once did. But all Minna's mother liked to do was write.

—from *The Facts and Fictions of Minna Pratt,* an ALA Notable Children's Book by Patricia MacLachlan

- If you were Minna, what would you tell your mother about her behavior?
- What can you do if you want your parents to act differently?

Journal entry for January 12
Kids understand that if it feels good, tastes good, sounds good, or looks good on them, their parents won't like it.

—from *The New One* by Jacqueline Turner Banks

- List some things that you like that your parents don't like.
- Does this work the other way, too? Do your parents like some things that you dislike? Make a list of them. Then compare your lists.

"They just want to keep you a baby all your life. Suds, I'm telling ya, you gotta put a stop to it now. If you leave it up to your mom, you'll be going off to college with a flying-elephant lunch box."

—from *Fourth Grade Rats* by Jerry Spinelli

- What are some of the things parents do to try to keep their kids young?
- How can children prove to their parents that they're not babies?

Mother's fried wontons turned out to be a hit at the bake sale. Listening to the other parents praise Mother's dish and watching her beaming face, I felt really proud of her. This was the first time I was proud of her being the way she was, instead of wishing she could act more like my friends' parents.

—from *Yang the Third and Her Impossible Family* by Lensey Namioka

- What are you proud of about your mother? Design an award for her. Be specific about her accomplishments.
- Yang and her family have moved to Seattle from China. Why do you think it's so important for Yang to feel that her mother fits in?

> *"You keep talking about everybody giving a little, Helen. Well, Dad is going to have to give a little, too. We'll do everything we can to make him know that we're glad to have him live with us, but I'm not about to change our whole life-style to please him. . . ."*
>
> —from *Racing the Sun* by Paul Pitts

- Because of ill health, Brandon's grandfather is moving from the Navajo reservation to live with his son in the city. Describe what kind of relationship you think Brandon's father and his grandfather have.
- List some of the adjustments that Brandon, his father, and his grandfather may have to make.

> *Junior High isn't elementary. The teachers and the principal have to look after a lot more kids. Or maybe there are more liars in junior high.*
>
> —from *True Friends* by Bill Wallace

- What do you think, are there more liars in junior high than in elementary school? Explain why you agree or disagree.
- Is lying ever justified? Give examples to support your answer.

> *My mother said that Grandmother Pickford's one act of defiance in her whole life as a Pickford was in naming her. Grandmother Pickford, whose own name is Gayfeather, named my mother Chanhassen. It's an Indian name, meaning "tree sweet juice," or—in other words—maple sugar. Only Grandmother Pickford ever called my mother by her Indian name, though. Everyone else called my mother Sugar.*
>
> —from *Walk Two Moons*, a Newbery Medal Book, by Sharon Creech

- If you were half Native American and half Anglo, would you want an Anglo name or a Native American one? Explain your choice.
- Why do you suppose it was considered an act of defiance for Grandmother Pickford to name her daughter Chanhassen?

"Your father and I have always given the best of everything to you. . . . But it means nothing to you. You've never really tried to learn your father's skill. You're not stupid. You could have if you'd tried. It wasn't exciting enough, I suppose, to be a puppet maker. You had to come here to where the applause and the money are."

"No, Mother, don't say that. I—"

"It will kill your father. He's not a healthy man—but you wouldn't have noticed."

—from *The Master Puppeteer* by Katherine Paterson

- What do parents owe to their kids?
- What do kids owe to their parents?

The beast my father roared especially ugly roars today. I never seem to please him, although it is true I never try. When I was a child, I ofttimes thought I was a foundling or, even better, the beloved daughter of our good king Edward.

—from *Catherine, Called Birdy*, a Newbery Medal Book, by Karen Cushman

- This passage is from the fictional diary of a girl who lived in the thirteenth century. How do her feelings relate to what kids feel like today?
- Why do you think the narrator never tries to please her father? What would you do if you were in her position?

> *"You talk like your dad is a real pain, and that's the way I always have felt about mine. But your dad looks like a great guy to me, so—well maybe mine could be too, if I gave him a chance. Your dad was saying I should."*
>
> —from *It's Like This, Cat*, a Newbery Medal Book, by Emily Cheney Neville

- Does it seem like the grass is sometimes greener on the other side of the fence? Are other kids' parents sometimes easier to talk to than your own? Relate a time when you felt this way.
- Who's the greatest guy you know? List the characteristics that make him, or her, so great.

> *For a long time after she arrived, Mrs. Post didn't pay any attention to anybody but me. She asked me how I liked school and what I thought about Schenectady and who my friends were and whether I was a Republican or a Democrat and how I felt about wearing secondhand clothes. Only two other people in the world had ever acted really interested in my ideas and my values before. One was Papa and the other was my fourth-grade teacher, Miss Simmons. (I still remember the day she asked me whether I thought George Washington was right or not when he refused to run for a third term as President. I don't know what I said, but it was great being asked.)*
>
> —from *Anywhere Else but Here* by Bruce Clements

- When adults ask you questions about your ideas and values, how do you feel? Do you think they're being nosy, or are you flattered by their interest?
- Who do you question about their ideas and values?

Pets and Other Animals

The cat was as gray as a mole and its fur was matted. As it peered toward the house, it shook its head constantly as though to clear away something that made seeing difficult.

"What's the matter with him?" Ned asked.

"Hunger," replied Mr. Scully. "No. Wait a minute. There is something wrong."

"One of its eyes is shut tight. . . . The eye isn't there," Ned said. "There's just a little hole." He felt a touch of fear. . . .

"You're right," Mr. Scully said. "The cold does that to them sometimes, and he looks big enough to have been born last year. Or else someone used him for target practice. A boy would do that. A living target is more interesting than a tin can."

—from *One-Eyed Cat*, a Newbery Honor Book, by Paula Fox

- Why do you think some kids do things to torture animals?
- In another place in the story, the hero asks, "Do bullies know they are bullies?" Write a paragraph to answer his question. Use any real-life experiences you might have.

"If you let me stay the night, I'll help you with your homework," Figment said in a muffled voice from beneath the bed.

"What does a dog know about homework?"

"Lots of things. I grew up watching 'Jeopardy' on TV. I can question you an answer on anything. . . I can do lots of stuff. I can answer the telephone. I can vacuum rugs. I can dust."

That's when Marcella heard the back door slam downstairs and her mother call out to her. "Can you pretend you're not even here?" Marcella said to the dog.

—from *Figment, Your Dog, Speaking* by Laura Hawkins

- Imagine a conversation between you and a pet or another animal. After you write down the conversation, act it out with a friend.
- If you had a dog like Figment, what would you like him to do to help you out around the house?

"If you ask me, that stupid sheep doesn't have any idea in the wide world what sort of animal it's supposed to be," said Joe.

"I think she's rather sweet," said Belinda.

"I don't," said Joe.

—from *Agnes the Sheep*, an Esther Glen Award Book and a Booklist Editor's Choice, by William Taylor

- It sounds as if Joe has definite ideas of what a sheep should be like. Describe your idea of what a sheep should be.
- What's the most unusual pet you've ever known or heard of that anyone had? Explain whether or not you'd be happy owning that kind of a pet.

When the dish towels were rinsed and hung in the sun, her mother said, "Go train your falcon, you'll learn a lot about birds . . . and yourself."

—from *The Summer of the Falcon* by Jean Craighead George

- What does the mother mean? How would training a young bird teach a child about herself?
- How does your treatment of your pet reveal things about you, especially about your good habits and your bad habits?

Soon as I see him, I know two things: (1) Judd Travers has taken his dogs out hunting, like he said, and Shiloh's run away from the pack, and (2) I'm not going to take him back. Not now, not ever . . . .

All I know right then is that I have to get Shiloh away from the house, where none of the family will see him.

—from *Shiloh*, a Newbery Medal Book, by Phyllis Reynolds Naylor

- What would you do if a dog you believed was being mistreated ran away and came to you?
- If you decided to keep the dog, how do you think your family would react?

I'd better start at the beginning of my story. My name is Huey, short for Hubert. I'm six years old and I live in New York City with Fred and Maureen Walton.

I have stubby legs, a longish body, an extremely large and sensitive nose, and very droopy eyes that always look sad.

I am a basset hound.

—from *Taxi Cat and Huey* by Gen LeRoy

- Write the opening page of your pet's autobiography. If you don't have a pet, write the autobiography for a pet you'd like to have.
- Draw a picture of an animal. Exchange pictures with a friend. Then write a description of the animal that your friend drew. Share your descriptions.

"Mark, come here. Now sit down, be quiet, and listen carefully. You know the trouble we're in with the whole town over Ben. They've demanded that we get rid of him or shoot him."

"Not shoot him!" Mark cried. "Not shoot Ben, Mother!"

"We won't have to if Arnie Nichols takes him out and turns him loose on an island. Don't you see? Ben will stay alive and free. Think what that means, Mark."

"But I can't lose him!" Mark cried.

—from *Gentle Ben*, a Sequoyah Children's Book Award Winner and an ALA Notable Book, by Walt Morey

- Why might people be opposed to someone in their town having a brown bear as a pet? How do you think you would feel?
- Can you imagine any other solution to Mark's dilemma? Explain your solution.

Fanny had wanted a dog all her life. . . . Fanny sensed that from the moment she was born she was meant to have a dog. It was as though some unique and independent organ deep inside her, like a tiny heart, couldn't thrive properly without one.

Henry's resistance to owning a dog was just as strong as Fanny's desire. The more she pleaded for one, the more emphatic Henry's refusals became. He lectured her on the troublesome aspects of training a puppy, emphasizing how time-consuming and filthy the whole undertaking was. None of the sermons convinced Fanny of anything except how stubborn her father was.

—from *Protecting Marie* by Kevin Henkes

- List all the pros and cons you can think of for owning a particular pet.
- Now take the dog's point of view. Imagine that a puppy wants to go home with Fanny. An older dog tries to convince the puppy that children don't make good owners. Create a dialogue between the two animals.

"Well, you be careful. Don't you get too close to those owls, you hear? You do and they're sure to come at you, and they can draw blood. . . . People are people, Brad, and owls are owls. They've got their own rules. . . ."

I'm out in the barn checking out those eggs every day. I talk to Mr. and Mrs. Christie. They answer me with sneezing and snoring sounds. At least I think they're answering me. Maybe they're just sneezing and snoring.

I'm probably keeping them awake. After all, owls are supposed to sleep in the daytime.

—from *Hey There, Owlface* by Betty Bates

- How might the rules of owls and people differ? What rules might they have in common?
- Explain whether or not you think it's possible for people to learn to understand owls—and to communicate with them.

We see our cat every day but from a distance. He won't eat if we're close by, but he knows us. I think he can tell time, because there he is, at the rescue rock at about three-thirty every afternoon. I get there first, wait for Sam, and when he shows up, like magic, there's the cat. Don't you think that's smart?

I'm so impatient for him to let us get close. I so want to pet him. Maybe he'll never let us and it will always be one-sided. Just us liking him and being shut out like from everything else here.

—from *The Broccoli Tapes*, a Booklist Editor's Choice Book and a Notable Children's Book in the Language Arts, by Jan Slepian

- Have you ever tried to make friends with an animal who was scared of you? Share your experience.
- Do you think cats are smart? Present evidence to back up your opinion!

I guess I called him Strider because there is a track club called Bayside Striders, and Strider seemed like a good name for a running dog. . . .

—from *Strider* by Beverly Cleary

Jim Ugly was a big sandy mongrel, part elkhound, part something else, and a large helping of short-eared timber wolf. . . . He might yip or bay or wolf-howl, but mostly he was silent. I'd never seen such a quiet, keep-to-himself dog. You just never knew when he was going to behave like a dog or like a wolf.

Dad never got around to naming him. He had just called the dog Amigo, which means "friend" in Spanish, and sometimes Jim Amigo, but I never called him that. The mongrel never much liked me and I never much liked him, and out of spite I hung the name Jim Ugly on him.

—from *Jim Ugly* by Sid Fleischman

- Take a survey of pet names. Find out what kinds of pets people have, what they call them, and why they chose those names.
- What name would you give Jim Ugly? Tell why you chose that name.

The fox came straight toward the grove of trees. She wasn't afraid, and I knew she had not seen me against the tree. . . . Her steps as she crossed the field were lighter and quicker than a cat's. As she came closer, I could see that her black fur was tipped with white. It was as if it were midnight and the moon were shining on her fur, frosting it. . . .

I thought about a newspaper with just one word for a headline, very big, very black letters, twelve inches high. FOX! And even that did not show how awesome it had really been to me.

—from *The Midnight Fox*, a Library of Congress Children's Book of the Year, by Betsy Byars

- Write a newspaper article about the most amazing animal sighting you've ever had.
- How do you think the fox would respond when it saw the narrator? Write a few paragraphs about the fox's reaction.

The snarling of the badger died away and was replaced by a low, curious whining. Ben made the same sound, watching the animal closely. Strangely, now that it was daylight he no longer felt so afraid of the creature. He looked curiously at that broad, white-streaked head, at the intelligent eyes studying him so close to his own face and he saw no sign of fear there, no indication of intent to attack. There was only a sort of returned curiosity about this diminutive human being in the burrow.

—from *Incident at Hawk's Hill*, a Newbery Medal Book, by Allan W. Eckert

- Which animals seem most intelligent to you? Relate how they show their intelligence.
- Explain why animals seem so much more dangerous at night to people.

As my father said, Wol never quite realized he was an owl. Most of the time he seemed to think he was people. At any rate, he liked being with people and he wanted to be with us so much that we finally had to stop trying to keep him out of the house. . . . He was always very well mannered in the house, and he caused no trouble—except on one particular occasion.

—from *Owls in the Family* by Farley Mowat

- Which kinds of pets are better suited to living inside? Which are better suited to living outside? Explain how you decided which kind of pet belonged inside or outside.
- Do you have a story about a well-mannered pet that "caused no trouble—except on one particular occasion"? Tell what happened.

When wolves killed it was usually in brutal fashion, at least by some human standards—a slow and tearing death. A pulling down and closing off of life.
But later John realized that there wasn't a right or wrong way about wolves hunting and killing the deer. There was just the wolves' way. That was the way they were and had nothing to do with what man thought was right or wrong.

—from *Tracker* by Gary Paulsen

- Talk about the different needs of animals and the values of people.
- Do you believe that a wolf could be trained to go against its natural instincts? Explain why, and tell whether or not you think that that would be right.

The Doctor is a huge, silver-gray tomcat. He is everybody's favorite alley cat. Even people who don't ordinarily like cats like The Doctor. Most everyone on Burnridge has tried to get The Doctor to be a pet by inviting him in and bribing him with chicken livers or tuna fish or chunks of hamburger. The Doctor is always a gentleman. He eats his meal, says his thanks, takes a nap, and asks to be let out. The Doctor is his own cat.

—from *Tails of the Bronx* by Jill Pinkwater

- What does the last sentence in the passage mean?
- If you were a cat, would you rather be like The Doctor or would you rather have a permanent home with someone? Give at least three reasons for your preference.

 "It is hungry, the little one," she said, petting the small raccoon. "Go fetch a clean wheat straw, Oscar."

She filled her own mouth with warm milk, put the wheat straw between her lips, and slanted the straw down to the mouth of the little raccoon. I watched, fascinated, as my new pet took the straw eagerly and began to nurse.

"Look how the little one eats," Oscar's mother said. "This is the way you will have to feed him, Sterling."

—from *Rascal*, a Newbery Honor Book, by Sterling North

- If you took care of a wild animal such as a raccoon, would you want to keep it or release it back into the wild when it was stronger? Explain why the wild or your home would be the better place.
- What would you do if you found a small animal that had been injured or abandoned?

 *Cloyd let Cocoa and Brownie maul him and pummel him and crawl all over him, just as their mother had let them. He talked to them with words and a stream of noises he could make with his lips. The bears learned fast that the skin on his hands was not as tough as his fur-covered body and that he didn't like it if they were too rough with their needle-sharp teeth. Soon they knew his moods and his warnings and his commands from the tone of his voice. They could tell when he was playing and when he wasn't. They couldn't touch his face with tooth or claw, but if he turned sideways, it was a signal he would allow a quick lick with the tongue.*

—from *Beardance* by Will Hobbs

- How would you feel about letting a bear lick your face?
- In your opinion, should—or could—a wild animal like a bear ever be turned into a pet? Give at least three arguments to support your opinion.

 *"I understand you're the owner of a live dinosaur. Well, I'm the vice-president of the Old Mill Pond Whiskey Corporation. I have a little proposition for you. I'd like to rent your dinosaur for a while, so we can use it in our big advertising campaign. . . . We'd pay you two hundred dollars a month while he lived. He'd last long enough to make good money out of him."*

—from *The Enormous Egg* by Oliver Butterworth

- What would you do if you had a dinosaur egg and a triceratops hatched from it? Advise the dinosaur owner in the passage above whether or not to take the Old Mill Pond Whiskey Corporation's offer.
- In the book and movie Jurassic Park, humans were able to bring dinosaurs to life. If scientists could really do that, explain whether or not you think they should.

Responsibility

It was a nice day until Mrs. Hanson couldn't find the Scholastic Book Club money. She was scrabbling around at her desk during reading. . . . Finally she interrupted the class. "Did anyone see a large manila envelope on my desk?"

No one answered.

"What was in it?" Jack asked.

"All the book money you students turned in. I was going to mail the order today, and I'm ready to count the money. The envelope was right here on my desk this morning. Does anyone remember seeing it?"

"Elsie sat at your desk when she was playing nurse," Jack said. . . .

Mrs. Hanson stood there thinking. She obviously didn't know what to do.

"I didn't take the money," Elsie announced loudly.

"Sure you didn't," Jack said . . . .

Mrs. Hanson asked Elsie to stay a minute after the class was dismissed.

—from *Nothing's Fair in Fifth Grade*, Winner of 13 state awards, by Barthe DeClements

- Although Jack didn't see Elsie take anything, as all the children know, Elsie once stole money out of their desks. Evaluate Jack's behavior. For instance, was he right to voice his suspicions? Was he being responsible or irresponsible?
- Mrs. Hansen makes Elsie clean out her desk. What would you have done if you were the teacher? Continue the passage by writing a scene between Mrs. Hansen and Elsie.
- How would you feel if you were Elsie and everyone believed that you had taken the money?

I, Amber Brown, am being held captive by a madwoman.

That madwoman is my mother and she's very mad at me for having a messy room.

She's also very mad at me because my teacher sent home a note saying I'm "not working up to the best of [my] ability."

—from *Amber Brown Wants Extra Credit* by Paula Danziger

- What does it mean for you when you work up to the best of your ability?
- What do you do that turns your mother into a "madwoman"?

Amy was proud of all the things she could do all by herself now that she was bigger.

She could braid her own hair, and most of the time it turned out okay. She could rollerskate and she could read better. She could go to the corner mini Mart alone.

But there were other things she still wanted to do. One of them was to babysit herself.

—from *Alone at Home* by Barbara Shook Hazen

- Make a "responsibility timeline," marking off mileposts of what kids should be responsible for at certain ages.
- Name at least five things that you're responsible for now. Then name at least five things you think you should be able to do now.

Aunt Gerda wasn't there to meet us when we got off the airport bus at the hotel.

"Where is she, Matt?" Abby asked. . . . I heard the edge of panic in her voice. . . . It must be hard to be five years old, to have no mom, to be in a strange place with only your not-very-big 13-year old brother to keep the scaries away. I was having a problem keeping the scaries away myself.

—from *The Ghost Children* by Eve Bunting

- No one expects a five-year-old to travel alone, to take care of herself or himself. At what age should a child be able to take care of herself and himself—and even be responsible for someone else?
- What would you have done if you were in Matt's position?

"Calvin," Mom had said, "I don't think you could care for a pet. I just had to remind you about homework. What if you forgot to feed your dog?"

"He would bark," said Calvin, "to remind me."

"Like I bark about your homework?" said Mom.

—from *Jazz, Pizzazz and the Silver Threads* by Mary Quattlebaum

- Is this a fair comparison—comparing homework with feeding a dog? Tell why or why not.
- How can kids prove to their parents that they are responsible?

Miss DeBoer was like an icicle when we spoke after class. She told me how disappointed she was in me. How could a smart boy and a good boy like you do something like this? she wanted to know. I had no answer for her, no answer she would like, anyway. Because I knew the truth.
I did it because I thought I could get away with it.

—from *Mostly Michael*, Winner of the Dorothy Canfield Fisher Award, the Mark Twain Award, and the William Allen White Award, by Robert Kimmel Smith

- If you don't get caught for being irresponsible, does that mean you're responsible? Explain your reasoning.
- What do you think the narrator did to make Miss DeBoer so angry?

I knew something was wrong the moment the door swung open. He'd sinned. Splinters of wood were all over the floor. He'd tried to chew his way out. Chunks of wood had been torn from the back of the door. Teeth marks were also on the door handle where he'd tried to open it. Splinters were on the sill and floor by the kitchen window. Tuck had been a one-dog wrecking party while I was in school.

—from *The Trouble with Tuck*, an Iowa Children's Choice Book and a California Young Reader Medal Winner, by Theodore Taylor

- Parents often say a child can't have a dog or a cat until he or she can be responsible for the animal. Tell why you think this is fair or unfair.
- In your opinion, who is at fault—the dog or the narrator?

I started to eat another cookie. There were exactly three chocolate pieces in it. "Do you know what I'm going to do when I get married?" I said. . . . "I'm going to make Toll House cookies with a hundred chocolate pieces in each cookie, and then I'm going to sit down and eat them all myself.

—from *Eighty-Eight Steps to September* by Jan Marino

• What do you want to do when you have your own home and are in charge of your life?
• Evaluate the narrator's plan for the future in terms of responsibility.

Junior had not been as sorry to see Monday come as he had thought. Pap had been right about Scooty [the hamster]. The whole thing was to teach responsibility, and Junior did not want any more lessons in that.

He would be glad to—well, he would be willing to—take lessons in reading and writing and spelling, even arithmetic. But he did not want any more lessons in responsibility.

—from *Wanted . . . Mud Blossom,* an Edgar Winner and an ALA Notable Book, by Betsy Byars

• What makes lessons in responsibility more difficult than lessons in reading and arithmetic?
• Why would taking the class hamster for a weekend be a lesson in responsibility?
• Share a lesson in responsibility that you've experienced.

The only people who do dumber things than seventh-grade girls, I decided, are seventh-grade boys.

—from *Alice In-Between* by Phyllis Reynolds Naylor

• What does the author mean? Give examples to prove—or disprove—her point of view.
• What is the dumbest thing that you've ever done? What, if anything, did you learn from doing it?

He sat in his room that night and started a list:

> *Gun*
> *Food*
> *Sleeping gear*
> *Four pairs of socks*
> *Four pairs of underwear*
> *Two shirts*
> *Three pairs of jeans*
> *Toothbrush*
> *Three months*

The last thing on the list seemed to write itself. Three months. He was going to be alone with the sheep for the rest of June, July, and August, until the first week of September.

I'll go crazy, he thought. Nuts. I don't even know what to do, how to do anything. How can Cawley teach me? Seven, eight days and he's supposed to teach me how to take care of six thousand sheep for three months?

—from *Haymeadow* by Gary Paulsen

- How would you feel if you had to learn how to take care of six thousand sheep in seven or eight days?
- Describe the biggest and most difficult responsibility you've ever had to handle.

Joshua Nelson was thrashed in school. What he had done was not half so bad, or so Teacher Holt explained, as that he sought to put the blame on another scholar. After the thrashing he had to write, "To thine own self be true" on foolscap one hundred times. (It is from a play by Mr. William Shakespeare who, Teacher Holt explained, lived and wrote in England, 1564-1616.) "To thine own self be true." Teacher Holt believes that very much; and so do I, I think.

—from *A Gathering of Days*, a Newbery Medal Book, by Joan W. Blos

- What do you think of these punishments for a student who misbehaves today?
- If you were a teacher, what kind of punishments would you use in your classroom?
- What does "To thine own self be true" mean?

"My mother has taught me reading and numbers," I answered as sharply as I dared.

"But who is to teach you how to think?" she snapped back.

—from *The Slave Dancer*, a Newbery Medal Book, by Paula Fox

- You have learned to read and count in school. Where did you learn to think? Who taught you?
- What is the difference between being able to read and compute and being able to think?

The four-thirty bell clanged the house awake. From every direction, Lyddie could hear the shrill voices of girls calling to one another, even singing . . . Her stomach rumbled, but she ignored it. There would be no breakfast until seven, and that was two and a half hours away. By five the girls had crowded through the main gate, jostled their way up the outside staircase on the far end of the mill, cleaned their machines and stood waiting for the workday to begin.

—from *Lyddie* by Katherine Paterson

- Today in this country we have child labor laws, protecting children from such work conditions. Compare your typical morning to Lyddie's.
- Would you rather be working than going to school? Explain why or why not.

Yes, Nacho knew what a vegetarian was, and at that moment, as he opened his math book and licked his pencil preparing to do division, he decided to become one. Mrs. Wigert was right, he thought. We must save the planet in small ways.

—from *Local News* by Gary Soto

- How will Nacho's becoming a vegetarian help save the planet?
- List some other "small ways" that can help the environment.

What's in a Name?

> *"Galadriel Hopkins. What a beautiful name! From Tolkien, of course."*
> *"No," muttered Gilly. "Hollywood Gardens."*
> *Miss Harris laughed a sort of golden laugh. "No, I mean your name—Galadriel. It's the name of a great queen in a book by a man named Tolkien. But you knew that."*
> *Hell. No one had ever told her that her name came from a book. Should she pretend she knew all about it or play dumb?*
>
> —from *The Great Gilly Hopkins*, a Newbery Medal Book,
>   by Katherine Paterson

- What are the advantages and disadvantages of having an unusual name like Galadriel?
- Look up the meaning of your name in a dictionary or a book about names. How does knowing the meaning affect your attitude about your name?
- Gilly is the nickname for Galadriel. Do you have a nickname? If so, share the story of how you got it. If not, make up a nickname for yourself.

> *I always thought I would feel more American if I'd been named Marjorie. I could picture a girl named Marjorie roller skating in America. (I had never roller-skated.) Or sled riding (there was neither snow nor hills in Hankow). Or being wild on Halloween night (I had never celebrated Halloween). The name Jean was so short, there didn't seem to be enough room in it for all the things I wanted to do, all the ways I wanted to be. Sometimes I wondered if my mother had picked a short name because she had her heart set on my being just one kind of person.*
>
> —from *Homesick: My Own Story*, a Newbery Honor Book, by Jean Fritz

- Jean Fritz grew up in China. How do you think that made her feel about her name? Do you believe that if her name had been Marjorie that she would have felt more like an American?
- Make an alphabetic list of one-syllable names, either boys' or girls'. Make an alphabetic list of three-syllable names, either boys' or girls'. Which list is more difficult to make, and why?

"He called me a zebra," I said. . . .

"A zebra is what they call kids who are half black and half white," said Anna. . . .

My heart knocked in my chest. "I never heard it in my old school," I said. "I think it's really stupid. Who does that little name-caller think he is?"

—from *The World of Daughter McGuire* by Sharon Dennis Wyeth

- There's an old saying, "Sticks and stones may break your bones, but names will never hurt you." Explain whether you agree or disagree with the saying.
- What prompts someone to call another person names?

"I'd like to start over. I've got to read. I can't stand not being able to read! Being Adam Zigzag!"

"What?" asked Dad.

"Sometimes I call myself . . . Adam Zigzag."

"Why on earth?" asked Mom.

". . . because everything I write looks nutty and squiggly. And my brain feels like that too."

—from *Adam Zigzag* by Barbara Barrie

- Give yourself a nickname that describes how your brain feels sometimes.
- Judge whether it's a positive or negative thing that Adam has given himself such a nickname.

I have always hated my name: Enid Irene Crowley. Now really. It would be a terrible name even for an old woman; for a fourteen-year-old girl it was unbearable.

—from *Taking Care of Terrific* by Lois Lowry

- Tell the story of how you got your name.
- How do you feel about your name? Does it feel older or younger than you are?

> *"Now, Miss Brownmiller," said the principal, "There must be a story behind your name as well. Don't tell me you're a witch."*
>
> *Salem laid her pencil down. "That's not far off, actually. My mother and father met each other in Salem, Massachusetts. My father says she bewitched him. He said he wanted his firstborn to be named Salem, whether it was a boy or girl."*
>
> —from *Report to the Principal's Office* by Jerry Spinelli

- Find out the name of the city where your parents met—and what your name might have been if they'd made the same decision as Salem's!
- List at least three first names you might give to your first child.

> *Aunt Jessie was a redhead, which is how she got her nickname Redbird from Uncle Nate, and because of her red hair she stood out from the rest of us.*
>
> —from *Chasing Redbird* by Sharon Creech

- How would you feel if you were Aunt Jessie and stood out from the rest of the family? For instance, would you appreciate or resent the nickname of Redbird?
- Do you have a nickname? If so, how do you feel about it?

> *A tall girl with teased hair edged in beside him and bumped him with her hip. "Move over, Shorty."*
>
> *Make me Air-Hair. Drew made a face. He swore if one more person so much as cracked a joke about his being short he was not going to be responsible for what he did next. What gave her and everyone else the right to keep bugging him about his height?*
>
> —from *The Shorty Society* by Sheri Cooper Sinykin

- Write at least three different responses that Drew could have made to the tall girl. Evaluate which response you think would have been most effective.
- Why do you think some people feel that it's all right to make fun of a person's height?

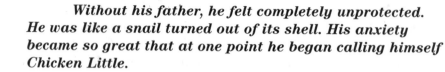

Without his father, he felt completely unprotected. He was like a snail turned out of its shell. His anxiety became so great that at one point he began calling himself Chicken Little.

"Oh, come on," Conrad would say, "it's going to be a nonviolent battle—just you and me and Parotti against the Fletcher brothers."

"Look, this is me you're talking to—Chicken Little," he would say, making a joke of his fear.

—from *Good-bye, Chicken Little* by Betsy Byars

- Discuss the pros and cons of giving yourself a bad nickname—before someone else does—such as Chicken Little.
- How do you feel when you're unprotected? Complete the following sentence: I am like _____ .

His grandmother had said that in the old days, people had a secret name that was known only to one other person—a name that described who they really were, not who the world thought they were. He had thought he would like to have such a name for himself, but this naming was no longer done. "I'll take a name for myself," he thought, eyeing the stone in his hand. "I don't need a father; I don't need anyone." Then he said aloud, "My name is Lone Bear."

—from *Bearstone* by Will Hobbs

- Why do you suppose that people have naming ceremonies for themselves?
  How do people benefit from secret names?
- Think of a name that describes who you really are.

When Al turned fourteen last month, she went into a tailspin. She decided Al was a babyish name. Plus it lacked class and pizzazz.

—from *Al's Blind Date* by Constance C. Greene

- Discuss whether or not people need different names at different times in their lives.

The cats all followed him into the kitchen as he started taking things out of the bag. They started mewing and rubbing against his legs as he took kidney after kidney out of the bag.

"There now, children," he spoke to them gently. He always spoke very softly. "There now. We're all going to eat now. Hello, everybody—yes, yes, hello. Hello, David, hello, Rasputin, yes, Goethe, Alex, Sandra, Thomas Wolfe, Pat, Puck, Faulkner, Cassandra, Gloria, Circe, Koufax, Marijane, Willy Mays, Francis, Kokoschka, Donna, Fred, Swann, Mickey Mantle, Sebastian, Yvonne, Jerusalem, Dostoievsky, and Barnaby. Hello, hello, hello."

—from *Harriet the Spy* by Louise Fitzhugh

- Collect the names that people give their cats. Find out why they chose those names.
- The cats are named after famous people. Do you know who Thomas Wolfe, Willy Mays, and Goethe were? Find out why these people are famous today.

"You'll be wanting a proper name, now that you're of age." It was half a question, half a statement of fact. "Have you chosen one?"

The boy shook his head. "I don't have any experience in such things," he mumbled shyly.

"Perhaps you. . . ."

"No, no." The swordsmith waved his chopsticks. "You must choose. It is your name, and it must please only you. . . ."

For several days he thought again about his name—the one he would carry and give to his children. He took out and examined again all the grand names he had once considered, but now they seemed pompous and unsuitable. He was what he was. No other name would change that.

—from *The Sign of the Chrysanthemum* by Katherine Paterson

- How do our names affect who we are?
- Why do you think the swordsmith insisted that the boy must choose his own proper name?

I frowned, trying to phrase the question carefully. "How did you get your name? Did your family visit Cuba?"

"Nope. I was named after my daddy's favorite type of cigar. He's told that story to the whole town." Havana seemed resigned to the fact.

I couldn't think of anything else to say but "Your father has quite a sense of humor."

—from *The Star Fisher*, a Christopher Award Book, by Laurence Yep

- Express your opinion about Havana's father's sense of humor.
- If you were Havana, would you tell the truth about your name or would you make up a different story? Either discuss why you would tell the truth or share the story you would make up.

"They called me that last week," she said. "Anastamosis Krupnik. And it was Steve who started it. . . ."

"Anastasia?" Sam said. "Can I say something? I want to say something really helpful."

"Okay."

"You could call Steve something bad. Then he'd know how it feels."

—from *Anastasia on Her Own* by Lois Lowry

- What do you think of Sam's suggestion?
- What advice would you give Anastasia?

Last year when David Bernstein was in third grade, there had been three other boys named David in his class. . . . David Bernstein did not like that a bit. It was much too confusing. Then, one day when he was reading a book called The Arabian Nights, *he discovered a wonderful name: Ali Baba. There were no other Ali Babas in his class. And as far as David Bernstein knew, there were no other Ali Babas in his school. It was the perfect new name for a boy who wanted to be different.*

—from *Hurray for Ali Baba Bernstein* by Johanna Hurwitz

- What's the most popular name in your class?
- Would you rather have a popular name or an unusual name? Share your reasons.

My name is Stepan Bakaian, or Step for short. I've been called Bak also, which isn't as cool, but it's better than Steven, which is my "American" name, given to me in first grade by that old battle-ax Swanson. That's the grade when all the foreign kids got their American names.

—from *Asking the River* by David Kherdian

- Why do you think a teacher might want to "Americanize" a child's name?
- Why do you think Stepan resents his teacher's action?
- Look up a common name, such as John, and find out what the name is in other languages.

Mrs. Choquette, their homeroom teacher, ushered him to the front of the room the way she always did for all the new students. He stared at the floor.
"This is Yoon Jun Lee from Seoul, Korea," she said.
"He's a June Goon?" yelled Travis Jones, the class bully, from the back of the room.
A few kids snickered. Alice felt her face grow hot. She didn't want to have anything to do with a country that gave its people such strange names.

—from *If It Hadn't Been for Yoon Jun* by Marie G. Lee

- Alice was born in Korea but adopted as a baby by an American couple. Why do you think she reacts to Yoon Jun's name the way she does?
- How would you respond to Travis Jones if you were Mrs. Choquette?

There are some people who don't look at home in their names. Not their real names, nor the names they invent for themselves. And Aunt Lucy was one. Her real name was Lucy Farr. Which I think is pretty nice. You know—Farr, distance, horizons, all that. But Aunt Lucy had no sense of horizons.

—from *The Genie of Sutton Place* by George Selden

- Think about names that fit people's occupations. For example, what should a chef's last name be? Hint: One way to get started is to look at names in the phone book.
- Are you "at home" in your name? Tell why or why not.

"When people say Okie they don't just mean people from Oklahoma."
Spence laughed shortly. "You're shorely right 'bout that," he said. "When Californians say Okie they mean dumb and dirty and lazy and most everthin' else bad they can think of."

—from *Cat Running* by Zilpha Keatley Snyder

- "Okie" was a term that referred to a migrant agricultural worker in the 1930s, particularly one who came from Oklahoma. We don't hear the term much any more. What names do people use today to refer to other groups of people, names that suggest something negative? For example, what does the word *alien* mean?
- What stereotypical ideas do you think people from other states might have about someone who lives in your state?

 *Like most Eskimos, Julie had two names,
English and Eskimo—Julie Edwards and Miyax
Kapugen. Hearing her father call her Miyax made her
feel closer to him, and she decided she would let only
him call her that. That name bound the two of them
to her mother, who had given it to her, and to each other. To the rest of the
people she would be Julie.*

—from *Julie* by Jean Craighead George

- What do you think about having two names, one private name for the most special person in your life and the other public name for everybody else?
- How does a name bind you to another person?

---

*The way all the kids said the name made it sound like "L-O-D." Like,
one, two, three, L-O-D. Cammy never knew to call her cousin anything but L-
O-D, which, she found out in school, was spelled E-l-o-d-i-e, Elodie. She'd
never stopped to think that cousin Elodie might have other names. Elodie
was just Elodie, like Cammy was Cammy. That, until a few months ago,
when her mama said something about Elodie's name being Eloise Odie.*

—from *Cousins* by Virginia Hamilton

- Eloise Odie's nickname is Elodie. Think of another way to shorten her name into a nickname.
- Have you ever been surprised to find out what someone's real name was? Or has someone been surprised to find out what your real name is? Share your story.

Word Wonder

Prance, I thought, liking the word. I am prancing. I am prancing in and out of the kitchen from the back porch, with my feet high in the air like a thoroughbred pony.

—from *Autumn Street* by Lois Lowry

- Substitute different words for the movement and the animal. If you used the word crept, for example, what phrase would you substitute for *like a thoroughbred pony*?
- Make a list of five words you like. Tell why you like the words.

Happy Valley. What a laugh. They should have called it Pathetic Molehill.

The Happy Valley Bungalow Colony was a collection of small, dirty-white, ramshackle cottages, some without indoor toilets or kitchens. . . .

—from *Summer Rules* by Robert Lipsyte

- Think about the names that people give things. For instance, look in a United States atlas or at a map for names of cities, towns, rivers, lakes, and mountains. Consider the street names in your own town. How accurate do you feel most of the names are?
- Write your own description of what a place named Happy Valley would be like.

"Why, my cabinet members can do all sorts of things. The duke here can make mountains out of molehills. The minister splits hairs. The count makes hay while the sun shines. The earl leaves no stone unturned. And the under-secretary," he finished ominously, "hangs by a thread."

—from *The Phantom Tollbooth* by Norton Juster

- Use a saying to describe what the duchess who is a cabinet member can do.
- Make a list of sayings such as "The early bird catches the worm." Explain what these expressions mean and why they're so appropriate.

 *She began the report by explaining the origin of the word halcyon. "The word halcyon," she wrote, "originated in Greek mythology. In those olden days of ancient Greece, halcyons were believed to be seabirds who built their nests on the ocean waves. These beautiful birds were so beloved by the gods that during their nesting season the gods stilled the winds and waves so that their nests would not be disturbed. This is why the word halcyon came to mean a time of beautiful peace and tranquility."*

—from *The Trespassers* by Zilpha Keatley Snyder

- Look up some of your favorite words in the dictionary to find out what their origins are.
- Use the word halcyon in your conversation or writing today.

"So tell me, Nick, why did you make up this new word, frindle?" asked Alice Lunderson.

Nick gulped and said, "Well, my teacher Mrs. Granger said that all the words in the dictionary were made up by people, and that they mean what they mean because we say they do. So I thought it would be fun to just make up a new word and see if that was true."

—from *Frindle* by Andrew Clements

- Make up a new word. Define what it means, what part of speech it is, and write a sentence using the word. Share your sentence with a friend and see if he or she can tell what your new word means.
- Explain what you think the word frindle means.

 *"I just happen to like three-letter words today. There are a lot of big topics with only three letters—God, for example, and Art, and bugs."*

"Bugs has four letters."

"Bug then. . . . There are more kinds of bugs than anything you know," he said, "except stars in the three-letter sky."

—from *Borgel* by Daniel Pinkwater

- What three-letter words can you think of? Which of these words describe big topics such as Art and God?
- Create a game where the players use only three-letter words.

Cassie sighed and smoothed over the letters with a sweep of her hand and wrote, I AM INFINITELY ANGRY. Cassie liked the word infinity. It was a big word with a big meaning. It was an i-n-f-i-n-i-t-e word.

—from *Cassie Binegar* by Patricia MacLachlan

- What is the biggest word you know? Rate the bigness of its meaning, using a scale of from 1 (little) to 10 (BIG).
- Can you remember a time when you were extremely angry? Like Cassie, describe your feelings by placing an adverb in the following sentence: I am (adverb) angry. Be as creative as you can. Discuss why you chose that particular adverb.

". . . promise is a meaningless word. People getting married promise each other to be happy forever. People promise to respect a certain idea forever. They must know these aren't things they can guarantee, no matter how much they want to. Sometimes I think the word is just useless. You can't promise anything that matters, and if it doesn't matter, why use such an important word."

—from *Noonday Friends*, a Newbery Honor Book, by Mary Stolz

- Express your opinion about the word promise.
- What was the last promise you made? Was it about something that mattered or about something that wasn't so important? Did you keep your promise?

> *"An enemy? What's that?"*
> *"That's hard to explain," I said again.*
> *"Make it short," he said.*
> *"An enemy is someone who wants to beat you up." I said that because I couldn't think of a better explanation, at least not if it had to be a short one.*
> *"Why does the enemy want to beat me up?" asked the Composgnathus.*
> *"Because he's an enemy."*
> *"And why is he an enemy?"*
> *"Because he wants to beat you up. That's logical."*
>
> —from *Dinosaur with an Attitude* by Hanna Johansen

- How would you explain to a dinosaur what the word enemy means?
- What other words are hard to define, even though we use these words all the time? Why are they so hard to define?

> *"I went down, you see, to show the King how far I've gone on my dictionary. He was pleased with the first part. He liked "affectionate is your dog" and "Annoying is a loose boot in a muddy place" and so on, and he smiled at "Bulky is a big bag of boxes." As a matter of fact, there was no trouble with any of the A's or B's and the C's were fine too, especially "Calamitous is saying no to the King." But then we got to "Delicious is fried fish" and he said no, I'd have to change that. He doesn't care for fried fish. The General of the Armies was standing there and he said that, as far as he was concerned, Delicious is a mug of beer, and the Queen said no, Delicious is a Christmas pudding, and then the King said nonsense, everyone knew the most delicious thing is an apple, and they all began quarreling. Not just the three of them—the whole court.*
>
> —from *The Search for Delicious* by Natalie Babbitt

- Can your class agree on a "Delicious is . . . " statement?
- Help the narrator finish the dictionary. Supply words and statements for the letters E through Z.

"Well, I call those kind of mosquitoes gallinippers. Gal-Ah-Nip-Pers. Gallinippers. . . ."

"Galla who? Well, look, Daddy, look at these." I showed him the big red bumps that had popped up on my shoulder. "Look what some gallathings did to me."

Daddy waved my bumps away. "Shoot, gallinippers can punch such big holes in your skin that you think they use knives and forks. I remember bites way worse than that. When I was a kid and the weather got cold, those gallinippers would drill holes through people's doors trying to get in, looking for heat and meat."

—from *Front Porch Stories at the One-Room School* by Eleanora E. Tate

- Give mosquitoes or another kind of pesky bug a new name. Then make up a tall tale about the mosquito or bug.
- What's your opinion of the word gallinipper? For instance, do you feel that it's a satisfying word? What does it express about mosquitoes?

We others, who have long lost the more subtle of the physical senses, have not even proper terms to express an animal's inter-communications with his surroundings . . . and have only the word "smell," for instance, to include the whole range of delicate thrills which murmur in the nose of the animal night and day, summoning, warning, inciting, repelling.

—from *The Wind in the Willows* by Kenneth Grahame

- Choose one of the senses besides smell. Be as creative and as descriptive as you can in defining that sense.
- What does the word smell convey to you? For instance, do you feel that it's a poor substitute for a "whole range of delicate thrills," or do you believe that it's a convenient way to express many things at once?

Other Reading

Adventure and Survival

The Door in the Wall
by Marguerite De Angeli

Calico Bush
by Rachel Field

Stone Fox
by John Reynolds Gardiner

Slake's Limbo
by Felice Holman

River Runners
by James Houston

Indian Captive
by Lois Lenski

Seven Spiders Spinning
by Gregory Maguire

Save Queen of Sheba
by Louise Moeri

Call It Courage
by Armstrong Sperry

The Swiss Family Robinson
by Johann Wysse

Being with Older People

Utterly Yours, Booker Jones
by Betsy Duffy

*Grand Mothers: Poems,
Reminiscences and Short Stories
about the Keepers of Our
Traditions*
edited by Nikki Giovanni

Toning the Sweep
by Angela Johnson

Sitti's Secrets
by Naomi Shihab Nye

The Cay
by Theodore Taylor

Dicey's Song
by Cynthia Voigt

Family Matters

It's Not the End of the World
by Judy Blume

Diary of a Frantic Kid Sister
by Hila Colman

Yolanda's Genuis
by Carol Fenner

Kevin Corbitt Eats Flies
by Patricia Hermes

No More Cornflakes
by Polly Horvath

Cave Under the City
by Henry Mazer

Fran Ellen's House
by Marilyn Sachs

Fitting In

Song of the Buffalo Boy
by Sherry Garland

The Fourth-Grade Celebrity
by Patricia Reilly Giff

The Frozen Waterfall
by Gaye Hicyilmaz

Family Pose
by Dean Hughes

Maizon at Blue Hill
by Jacqueline Woodson

Flights of Fantasy

Indian in the Cupboard series
by Lynn Reid Banks

A String in the Harp
by Nancy Bond

The Court of the Stone Children
by Eleanor Cameron

The Ear, the Eye, and the Arm
by Nancy Farmer

My Father's Dragon
by Ruth Stiles Gannett

Babe: the Gallant Pig
by Dick King-Smith

The Light Princess
by George MacDonald

Tom's Midnight Garden
by Phillippa Pearce

*Sailing to Cythera and Other
Anatole Stories*
by Nancy Willard

Friendship

Queen of the Sixth Grade
by Ilene Cooper

*Hello, My Name Is Scrambled
Eggs*
by Jamie Gilson

Daphne's Book
by Mary Hahn

Spring Break
by Johanna Hurwitz

Getting Even
by Mavis Jukes

Mrs. Fish, Ape, and Me, the Dump Queen
by Norma Fox Mazer

The Seventeenth Swap
by Eloise McGraw

Soup
by Robert Newton Peck

The Loner
by Esther Wier

Lots of Laughter

Mr. Popper's Penguins
by Richard and Florence Atwater

I'm Going to Be Famous
by Tom Birdseye

The Shrinking of Treehorn
by Florence Parry Heide

Ruthann and Her Pig
by Barbara Ann Porte

The Mysterious Disappearance of Leon (I Mean Noel)
by Ellen Raskin

How to Eat Fried Worms
by Thomas Rockwell

Freaky Friday
by Mary Rodgers

Parents, Teachers, and Other Adults

Just Like Martin
by Ossie Davis

The Cuckoo's Child
by Suzanne Freeman

The Sunita Experiment
by Mitali Perkins

Pot Luck
by Tobi Tobias

Pets and Other Animals

Sounder
by William H. Armstrong

National Velvet
by Enid Bagnold

The Incredible Journey
by Sheila Burnford

The Cat Who Went to Heaven
by Elizabeth Coatworth

Old Yeller
by Fred Gipson

Foxy
by Helen V. Griffith

The Jungle Book
by Rudyard Kipling

Gay-Neck: The Story of a Pigeon
by Dhan Gopal Mukerji

The Yearling
by Marjorie Rawlings

Where the Red Fern Grows
by Wilson Rawls

Dominic
by William Steig

A Sunburned Prayer
by Marc Talbert

Responsibility

The Half-a-Moon Inn
by Paul Fleischman

Niki's Little Donkey
by Coby Hol

Peace Tales: World Folktales to Talk About
by Margaret Read MacDonald

Down in the Piney Woods
by Ethel Footman Smothers

What's in a Name?

A Book about Names
by Milton Meltzer

When Joe Louis Won the Title
by Belinda Rochelle

Don't Call Me Marda
by Sheila Welch

Word Wonder

Alice in Wonderland
by Lewis Carroll

Bing Bang Boing
by Douglas Florian

Antics! An Alphabetical Anthology
by Cathi Hepworth

All Small, Little
by David McCord

All the Small Poems and Fourteen More
by Valerie Worth